Eldrid

COIN
collecting

FOR BEGINNERS

The Easy and Ultimate Guide for
Newbies to Start Your Own Coin
Collection From Scratch as a Fun
Hobby to Share With Family &
Friends or as a Profitable Business.

Writing a book was a hard challenge, but it was also more rewarding than I could have ever imagined. Nothing written in this book would have been possible without my colleague and friend John Hernandez. You gave me plenty of insights and you are a source of inspiration.

I'm also grateful to my uncle Tom who introduced me to the amazing world of coin collecting. Without his passion for this hobby, this book would never exist.

Lastly, a few words need to be dedicated to the best woman in the world, my wife Sophie who supported me from the first day and encouraged me to write this book and share my passion with as many people as possible.

TABLE OF CONTENTS

COIN COLLECTING FOR BEGINNERS

INTRODUCTION

WHY COIN COLLECTING?

Welcome to the world of coin collecting!

If you bought this book or if you have received it as a gift, it probably means that you want to learn more about coin collecting. I hope this is the case and that you are excited to discover the secrets and all the basics of coin collecting. If you are ready, let's start!

Several historians agree that coin collecting first started in Asia. People started to use coins as a way of exchange for goods and services by the time the Middle Ages began. It's not a secret that the first Chinese coins were made out of bronze while Roman coins were minted out of silver. The first coins minted in Europe were gold and silver double-struck pieces called bezants that were minted in the year 772 in Constantinople, which is now known as Istanbul, Turkey. These coins were used as an accepted form of currency until Gutenberg printed his own version of the book called "The Gutenberg Bible" which means that people would trade different versions for one or they used to buy their books with them as well. These coins were more easily accepted because the face on them was similar to the current coins that people used. The Byzantine Empire's currency was called "Tetraevangelia" which means "the four gospels". For this reason, it was thought that pieces of the face of Christ should be on them so it became a tradition for people to put his image on their coins. Around the year 919, Charlemagne minted an extremely valuable coin called a "solidus" which represented the gold content in an ounce and had a portrait of him on it saying "Patefim Sacrum."

Today, there are three basic types of coins: Minted coins, private-issue (such as state and municipal), and commemorative. Coins are made from five metals: copper, nickel, zinc, silver, and gold. The most usual type of coin is the silver coin minted by the US government which is called the American Eagle. Probably, this is also the coin that you are more familiar with. However, not all coins are minted in the US because some countries do not have a government in place to mint their own money. An example of this would be Canada, which issues their own coins with the face of Queen Elizabeth II on them or Australia, which issues them with a kangaroo. Another example that you were probably not aware of is Kuwait. Coins in Kuwait have pictures of the king along with several other symbols including camels.

I don't want to annoy you with a lot of history so I will keep it short. However, I really can't avoid telling you why coin collecting is also often referred to as "the hobby of the kings". The reason for this is that during The Renaissance time in the largest European countries such as France and Germany having a coin collection was extremely expensive and only wealthy and powerful families could afford to own a private coin collection. Today, you are lucky because you don't need to be a king (even if you feel you are) to start your own coin collection.

Today, coin collectors enjoy collecting, trading, and exchanging coins for many different reasons. Some people collect coins because it is a fun hobby, others do it for investment purposes and some even combine both of those reasons to collect coins. Some do it accidentally because they get fascinated by coins especially, from many generations back. Others take it very seriously and keep coins in order to preserve history. It is true that over the years, some coins are worth more than they used to be. However, every coin collector I spoke with during my life always struggles when they decide to sell their coins. This is the reason why one thing many coin collectors do with their old or expired coins is to donate them to charity or to family members as gifts.

Summing up, everyone starts to collect coins for their own reasons. Your reason is different from any other coin collector.

Personally, I love to collect coins because I love history, and being the owner of a coin makes me feel part of that frame. It's like traveling back in time without a time machine. Doesn't it feel great to have a coin that existed in the 1700s when you were not in existence? I don't know you, but I would feel like I was going back in time and experiencing the times of Abraham Lincoln.

Before starting with the nitty-gritty of coin collecting, let's have a more detailed look at the most common reasons why people do start coin collecting. I hope that before starting your coin collection you have already decided your reason to start. If not, you should start to think about it now.

Which category do you fall in?

Collecting as an Investment

Some collectors are after coins for their monetary value. These collectors look for high-quality, rare and in-demand coins that can fetch high prices among numismatic connoisseurs. This is because there are coins made of valuable metals such as silver and gold; others are rare and may be sold for millions of dollars. The current most valuable coin is the 1907 Saint-Gaudens Double Eagle which is worth $7 million US. Yes, you read right: $7 million US.

If it's your primary goal to sell off your coins you will need to do a lot of research about coins to learn their value, the materials particular coins are made of, and keep up with market trends to know which ones are on demand. This will enable you to make smart acquisition decisions so that you can have a great investment. Keep in your mind that you might have to buy most of these valuable coins.

It is important to understand that you may not get a return on your investment immediately or within the next ten years. If you are in this, brace yourself to be in it for the long haul. If you are making smart decisions on your acquisitions now, you will have great returns in the future.

John J Pittman Jr., the famous coin collector and numismatist, assembled a world-class coin collection over many decades. He searched for exceptional coins, high in value and rare that he could afford, and added them to his collection. In 1997, David W. Akers sold this exceptional coin collection for 30 million dollars! In this collection was a proof 1883 Capped Head gold five-dollar half eagle coin, which he bought for $635 in 1954. In 1997, it had increased in value and sold for $467,500! Imagine that. So much profit was made and all because of one valuable thing that John applied when collecting coins as an investment, which is Knowledge. You have got to know your coins.

If you decide to start coin collecting as an investment you should really become an expert and become able to spot the value of a coin. In the past, coin collectors have given up their possession of coins due to the fact that they could no longer afford them or because inflation caused a drastic change in their values. It is for these reasons that several people give up on their hobby and turn to other things they enjoy now. It is not uncommon for someone to collect coins and then lose interest before realizing that there was a huge increase in value from what they had originally collected. Inflation can cause serious problems for coin collectors as well as people who own stocks or bonds.

Coin collecting is similar to every other investment. They depreciate in worth, and other coins may experience an uphill climb. The ideal method to profit from coin collecting is to be up-to-date with the news and the routine coin prices. This will assist you not to be deceived by numerous merchants but to help in finding out how to price a coin even without a catalog.

Collecting coins for investment can also be dangerous because some coins are highly demanded and fake copies are made, some counterfeiters have been caught by the government before and have been held accountable for the distribution of such counterfeit coins. Don't worry; in this book, I will give you some tips to help you to spot fake coins and prevent scams.

To Learn About History

Some people collect coins to document history. Imagine holding in your hands a 1943 US penny made of zinc-coated steel other than the usual copper they use nowadays, or an ancient coin with a portrait of earlier century leaders such as Alexander the Great. It's cool to have pieces of history with you. It's evidence of the existence of generations before us and shows us just how far we have come. It takes you back in time when you were not in existence. It is fascinating to be a historical coin collector.

These people collect coins by date, mint mark, country of origin, condition (scratched or not) and a variety of other factors. They love to categorize them into collections like commemorative coins for any specific event such as the Olympic Games or Winston Churchill's birthdays with their family crest on it or specific medals and tokens for sports championships. There are thousands of coins in circulation today and there are many different types of coins in circulation. There are some very valuable dates or mintmarks, for example, the key date of the 1909 penny. A real key date is a coin that has a very low mintage compared to other dates and often has a higher value due to its rarity. An example of this would be the 1914-d Lincoln cent, which is also known as the Wheat Ear penny because it features an ear of wheat on its reverse side. Out of all the Lincoln cents produced in 1914, only 1% contained this wheat ear variety so it is considered to be a key date Lincoln cent, so it is worth more than 4 times its value than the regular Lincoln cent.

Here the focus is mostly on the calendar, which year the coin was made, any special event that was marked during that time, whose portrait is on it, and so on. Research it for the history behind each coin, which you can document and label on the coin case or wherever you choose to put them (We shall discuss more on proper coin storage).

As a Hobby; for Fun!

Some are in it for the thrill of assembling a collection. They may be excited to track down a rare coin, to finish a particular set of coins or they may be appreciating the artistic value of the coins.

If you are doing it for fun, it does not matter what coins you collect if they are orderly arranged in your collection. Throwing coins in a piggy bank is not making a collection. You need to arrange and classify your coins in a way that you can identify them and connect them with the reason they ended up in your collection. For instance, you can have a category for rare coins from the 18th century, new coins for the 20th century; the now 'extinct' zinc-coated steel coins, and so on. Other than that, collect whatever gives you that 'thrill'.

To Pass on to Future Generations

A coin collection could be one of the most valuable things you pass on to your kids. It could be your legacy, to live on even after you are gone. You see, if we could face reality, it looks like paper or coin money may not exist in the coming generations. People are already adopting crypto currency and other forms of intangible currency. Who knows, it may be what people use to transact business in the coming days.

How precious will tangible money in form of a coin collection then be? It will be a precious gift to own. Also, as coins increase in value over time, and their rarity in the coming days considered, your collection will be a gold mine. The coming generations may benefit greatly from your decision to start this hobby.

Whether for investment, as a way of documenting history, or as a hobby, coin collection is quite a fun activity for many people. Finding and owning those coins is going to bring you so much joy. You see, every coin that you manage to add to your collection is an achievement. It's exciting as well as fulfilling!

So, let us begin?

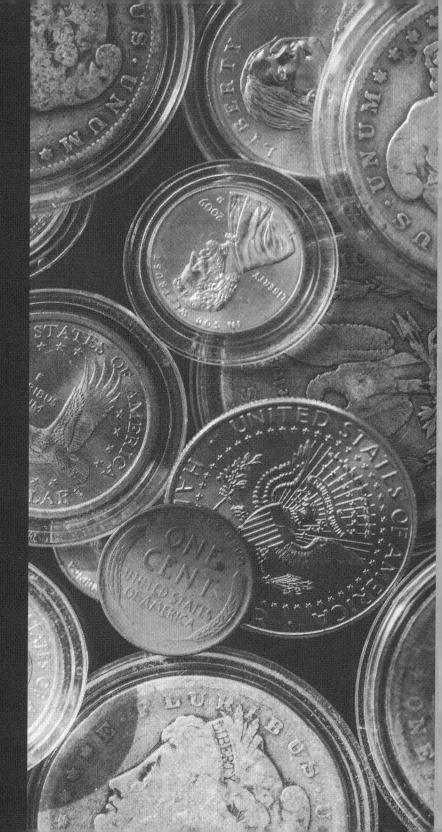

COIN COLLECTING FOR BEGINNERS

CHAPTER 1

STARTING WITH SOME LINGO

The first step to get started in the world of coin collecting is to learn the language. Learning coin collectors' terms will help you communicate easily with dealers, other numismatics, and coin collection enthusiasts. I really encourage you to take some time to carefully read the most common numismatic terms with a brief explanation of their meanings. Don't worry if you don't grasp all the definitions immediately, learning the language takes time and dedication!

TIP -> Once you have finished reading the book and you start with your first steps in coin collecting you can always go back to this chapter and use it as a glossary.

ANA (American Numismatic Association)

The biggest numismatic association for mint piece authorities. The ANA has the primary goal of studying and classifying cash while supporting the community of coin collectors across the US.

About Good (AG)

A flawed coin that shows substantial wear. The lowest evaluation assigned to a coin.

About Uncirculated (AU)

A flowed coin that shows just a limited quantity of wear on the high area(s) of the coin's plan, notwithstanding conceivable contact marks (pack marks). AU is the most noteworthy evaluation relegated to a circled coin.

Bag Marks

Small scratches appearing on a coin, at least uncirculated, caused by contact with other coins in a unique canvas package from the mint.

Bid/Ask

The offer cost is when a seller will pay for collectible coins. Ask cost is the value a merchant will acknowledge for the coin utilizing the spot cost as a source of perspective (see spread definition beneath).

Brilliant Uncirculated

An uncirculated coin has some mint gloss with no wear marks, yet some contact marks are available in at least one coin territory. These are generally connected with the lower Mint State evaluations of MS-60 to MS-62.

Bullion Coin

A penny whose significance varies atop the inbuilt valuation of the treasured metallic this one comprises.

Certified Coin

A coin that has been studied, ensured, and encased in a sealed plastic cover (a.k.a. "slabbed") by one of the perceived reviewing administrations (ANACS, NGC, PCGS, and so on).

Choice Uncirculated

A term commonly used to depict a coin studied MS-63, which means some contact marks are available.

Clad Coin

A coin characterized by one metal in the center and an external layer made of a different metal. Utilized by the U.S. Mint for circled coins starting in 1965.

Coin Grading

The way toward deciding how high or low a coin ought to be evaluated, considering wear checks and sack marks, among different elements.

Commemorative Coin

A coin delivered to perceive/commend an individual or function.

Counterfeit Coin

The multiplication or changing of a coin by somebody other than the authentic guarantor.

Die

The form of metal used to strike and produce a coin

Extremely Fine (EF or XF)

A coin with most of its mint lustre and few signs of beign circulated. Only a marginal wear can be seen when inspected closely.

Face Value

The money-related worth relegated and stepped on a coin (it can be not the same as the real worth is attached to the estimation of the metal it contains).

Fineness or Fine

The valuable metal level in a coin is compared with all the metals that make up the coin. For example, a fineness of .900 implies that 90% of the coin is silver and the rest composite.

Fine Weight

The genuine load of the silver contained in silver coins (rather than the gross weight, which incorporates the heaviness of the apparent multitude of coin's metals).

Fine (F)

An assignment of coin evaluating just underneath Very Fine (VF) where the coin has more than the reasonable wear of a VF coin. The plan shows sensible detail.

Gem Uncirculated

An uncirculated coin with few contacts denotes may not be noticeable to the unaided eye. Typically used to depict a coin evaluated MS-65.

Good (G)

A coin allocation that assesses where the coin has critical wear. However, the primary figures are still seen in great detail, but with no luck. The second-most minimal evaluation.

Gram

In the decimal standard, this is the fundamental unit of weight (31.1033 grams approaches one Troy ounce).

Intrinsic Value

The genuine estimation of the valuable metal (i.e., silver or gold) inside a coin dependent on the current spot cost.

Legal Tender

A coin that received approval by an administration or other public financial authority as a mode of trade. It can be utilized in the release of obligations.

Luster

The sheen or brightness of a newly printed coin brought about by the high weight applied when the coin is struck.

Market Value

The going cost of a coin on the open market (which might be equivalent to its inherent worth or more prominent).

Mint Mark

A letter image on a coin that recognizes where it was stamped.

Mint State

Used to portray a coin that has, for no reason, remained gushed and took not at all garb inscriptions. Mint conditions list beginning 60 throughout 70.

NGC (Numismatic Guaranty Corporation)

A few of the premier currency studying and validation establishments.

Numismatic Coin

A denomination whose value can be determined by absence, condition, strike, and request with a little accentuation on the metal estimate.

Obverse

The frontage of a coin that contains the fundamental image is also referred to as the "heads" sideways.

PCGS (Professional Coin Grading Service)

One of the most reputable organizations, which appraises and confirms coins.

Perfect Uncirculated

Undispersed penny that takes stay calculated MS-70, contemplating the "remarkable currency" (partaking not at all flaws).

Planchet

The clear (or coin plate) on which the kick the bucket engraves a coin's plan.

Premium

The sum over the spot value that the merchant charges coins so they can get a benefit and stay in business.

Proof

A coin created by uncommonly arranged bites the dust utilizing exceptional striking strategies bringing about a serious extent of detail and normally a mirror-like field (the zone encompassing the fundamental image(s)). Verification currencies are made explicitly for gatherers, not implied of course, and not permitted to interact with different coins at the mint.

Proof Set

A set comprising one proof coin of every category given by a mint for a particular year.

Reverse

The reverse side to the front is known as the "tails" side.

Spot Price

The current cost at which coins are utilized to set up purchasing and selling costs (see offer/inquire). It is sometimes mentioned as the "money cost".

Spread

The distinction between the purchasing cost and the approaching cost for a coin.

Uncirculated

A coin in new condition (as the mint has given it) that has not been set into dissemination.

Very Fine (VF)

An assignment of coin evaluating where the coin has light to direct even wear on the high regions of the coin yet much detail.

Very Good (VG)

The assignment for a coin that shows extensive wear with the primary highlights clear yet with a fairly straightened appearance.

Wear Marks

Denotes that show up on the high zones of the front and opposite of a coin because of the coin's course.

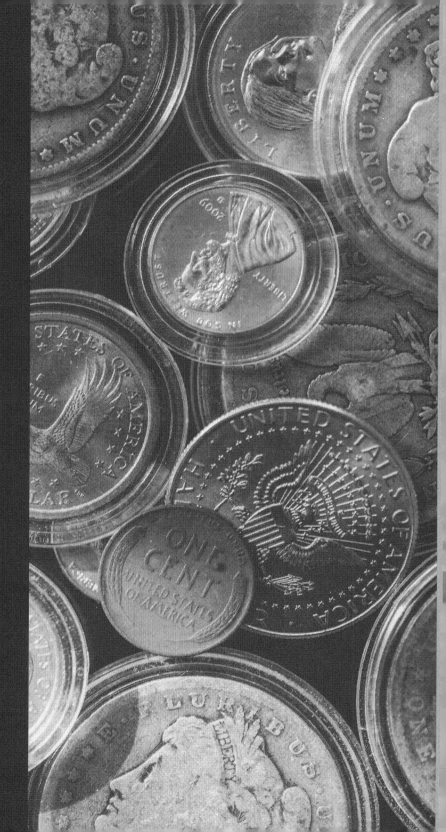

COIN COLLECTING FOR BEGINNERS

CHAPTER 2

LET'S TALK ABOUT US COINS

Popular Types of United States Coins for Beginners

If you are at the beginning of your journey with coin collecting, my advice is to start with coins that are not hard to find and they are not very expensive. Don't think that starting a coin collection means putting so much money on the table. My advice for you as a beginner is to start small and then you can use the first coins to build your collection from the ground up. In the next pages, you will find a series of coins that you can start collecting with small money and time from tomorrow.

Washington Quarters (50 States/ America the Beautiful Quarters)

The Washington Quarters are most known because they depict what is considered the most beautiful places in America. The Washington Quarter has acquired popularity from 1999 when the 50 State Quarters first debuted. They are appreciated by experts and beginners alike for their design, which has changed a lot over the years. I'm sure you know that the Washington Quarters are made of silver. Today these coins only have a small percentage of silver but between 1932 and 1964 the amount of silver within the coins was close to 90%. It's not a secret that the first American coin collectors started collecting these coins for their value. Some wanted to melt them to extract the silver. Today, most of the Washington Quarters don't have a lot of value, but you can certainly collect them if you appreciate their design. My advice is to start collecting the series that are circulating today and then start collecting the older versions going backwards by year. If you feel brave you can also decide to start collecting Washington Quarters from a specific decade.

TIP -> If you want to include kids or grandkids at the start of your coin collection you should definitely start from here!

Kennedy Half Dollars

The Kennedy Half Dollars are very popular in the US as well as abroad because they were made in honor of the 35th President of the United States John F. Kennedy who was assassinated in 1963. These dollars were first minted in 1964, the year after the tragedy. This coin is no longer in circulation so for you it will be more difficult to put your hands on one of them. However, it is legal tender and is still minted for certain collections. I think that it's a great commemorator of one of the most outstanding times in history and every coin collector should have one.

Lincoln Cents

The Lincoln penny is a versatile coin in American history. The first Lincoln cent was minted in 1909. The first editions of the coin represented a pair of wheat stalks. Since the first editions many versions and updates of the coins have been done and today there are hundreds of different versions. Luckily, some of these versions are currently in circulation so my advice is to start from them. Because they are considered "common" coins their value is generally not very high but this means that you can easily find different editions on E-bay or other online websites and marketplaces.

The Morgan Silver Dollars

The Morgan Silver Dollar is a large dollar coin, which features the head of Miss Liberty on the head and an eagle on the tail. It got its name from the engraver, George T. Morgan who designed it. Its minting officially started in 1878 through to 1921. It is quite an ancient coin. This coin was quite difficult to find but in 2021 the US government has minted the coin as a special non-circulating coin. This means from 2021 finding one of these coins has become easier and you might want to take advantage of that. This coin has 4 different mints with its own mark. Only Philadelphia does not have its own mark. If you are into coin collecting for the history behind them or their design, I don't recommend you to look for this coin but if you are looking for a good investment, this is probably your coin. The value of the Morgan Silver Dollar has increased across the years significantly and it could potentially grow more.

Commemorative Coins

A category of coins that I personally love and that I recommend you to consider is commemorative coins. As the name suggests, these coins are issued for a limited period of time to commemorate and honor a specific person, place, or event that was recognized as important.

Commemorative coins in the United States began to become popular in the 1930s when they were required by law to be minted by the United States Mint. They were sold to distributors who also added a premium on top of the actual value of the coin. However, this did not last for a long period of time, as collectors started to complain about speculators manipulating the prices and the market. As such, the US Mint started to produce fewer commemorative coins. Most of them are not made for circulation but in the United States, they are considered to be legal tender. Some of them tend to have a good monetary value especially if they are part of the "early commemoratives". If you are not looking for value but you want beautiful commemorative coins that are easy to find I really encourage you to start with the Washington Quarters (editions of 1932-1998). You may also collect them as proofs for events. Imagine yourself in the future saying "I was here when a certain event took place"

The first wave of commemorative coins attracted a lot of people into coin collecting, just as they are today as well. To date, commemorative coins are considered to be appealing and beautiful not only for collectors but even for people who don't have much to do with coin collecting in general.

If after starting collecting the first coins you understand that you are into commemorative coins, you should also consider collecting medallions. The word "medallion" is frequently used to describe a variety of types of coins but most of them are commemorative coins. As a general rule, "medallions" are pretty much any type of round, decorated piece of metal that has some sort of significance attached to it (such as monetary value, for example). You will soon learn that the main difference is that real medallions do not have legal tender attached to them while commemorative coins often have. This doesn't always apply, but it does for most currencies.

TIP: commemorative coins and medallions are often collected with revolutionary coins. As the name suggests, revolutionary coins are coins that circulated in times of revolution (such as the American Revolution of 1776, for example). Because of the historical significance they bear, these coins can be quite valuable (but this depends on other factors too).

Error Coins

As a beginner, a very intuitive way to start building your coin collection is by choosing coins that have one or more errors. Basically, these coins were manufactured with an error (such as a double denomination, overdate, or brokerage). They came out of the mint this way, and some might be tempted to believe they are not valuable at all. However, depending on the defect and depending on the era they came from, error coins can be quite pricey as well. We are normally used to the fact that when something has errors, it's bad and should be replaced. Well, this is definitely not the case. Most of the coins that have errors in their design are unique and have a lot of value. They are considered very rare and therefore also difficult to find.

If you decide to start collecting coins that have errors you don't usually follow a specific classification (country, year, etc.) but you just look for all the coins that are not "normal". To make this process easier you could think of starting from silver coins. The Kennedy Half Dollar would be a very good starting point.

If you are the kind of person that doesn't want to start with the easy coins but prefers to start big and look for the most valuable ones, you can find some inspiration from some high value error coins listed below. You will also find other "alternatives" to coins that you might want to consider if you are very curious.

Wrong Planchet

As the name suggests, a wrong planchet error is a coin stuck on a planchet. Some coins that you see stuck on a planchet are Lincoln Cents (before 1919 and between 1919 and 1940), but also the Shield Nickel, the Liberty Nickel, and the Buffalo Nickel. Others are: the Washington Quarter Silver, the Washington Quarter Clad, the Walking Half, and the Franklin Half. A fun way to start collecting the wrong planchet is by looking for the State Quarters available in your state. Most of the states have the wrong planchet.

Clipped Planchet

Clipped planchet are coins that appear to have a "bite" taken out, often due to a cutting error when they were being minted. Many beginners think that these coins are always rare and monetarily valuable, but this is not always the case. Indeed, you should look at three factors when assessing these coins: how important the clipped error is, the type of error, and the general status of the error. You can start looking for clipped planchet checking your pockets and looking for the coins you have around. The Jefferson Nickel, the Franklin Half Dollar, and Silver Roosevelt Dime are just some examples of coins that can present this error. If you decide to look for these particular coins don't buy anything online because there are many scams on these coins. Instead, visit a coin shop or get in touch with a coin dealer.

Souvenir Coins

These coins are quite interesting. Basically, they are normal coins that have been pressed, elongated, and redesigned. The most interesting fact about them is that mutilating coins with the purpose of putting them back into circulation again is illegal, with the exception of these souvenir pennies. Definitely a quirky addition to any collector's files!

Tokens

Trade tokens tend to be quite rare and very collectible. Sometimes, they can be worth as much as several hundreds of dollars (e.g., Civil War tokens, for example). Most often, these tokens were created in times of financial trouble when silver and gold were scarce, and yet people still needed something for their currency.

Tokens were usually valued at $1 or less at their face value, but there are tokens that can go as high as $5, for example. Just like "normal" circulated coins, they were used in everyday transactions.

Basically, these coins were manufactured with an error (such as a double denomination, overdate, or brokerage). They came out of the mint this way, and some might be tempted to believe they are not valuable at all. However, depending on the defect and depending on the era they came from, error coins can be quite pricey as well.

BU Rolls

BU Rolls are very representative of the new wave of coin collecting enthusiasts of the late 1950s and early 1960s. These "rolls" were bank-wrapped Brilliant Uncirculated small stashes of coins that made collectors go crazy in the era. Their 15-minute of fame started to fade out when collectors realized that, although some of these BU rolls were advertised as rare, they were, in fact, quite the opposite (as they had been manufactured by the millions). As such, BU Rolls tend to be shockingly cheap these days, so you might want to avoid falling into a trap on them.

Silver Certificates

Old Silver Certificates were used by people to redeem one silver dollar. However, these certificates were only valid up to 1964 when the government discontinued their manufacturing. For a while though, people were allowed to redeem their silver certificates for a given amount of silver, which eventually turned into a whole new craze in the coin collecting world as everyone was "suddenly" looking for these.

Clearly, just like other fads, this trend attracted a lot of people into the coin collecting world.

Art Bars

Somewhat an oddity, art bars were very popular in the 1970s. They were thin, rectangular silver bars weighing one ounce and they had polished surfaces and designs meant to commemorate pretty much everything you can imagine: from your wedding to your cat.

At first, mintages were limited, so art bars were very sought after. However, the market was flooded by a lot of these art bars, and eventually, people got bored of it. Like the other types of coins presented in our list which led to a new trend, art bars attracted a lot of collectors to the world of coins as well.

There's no actual right or wrong type of coin to collect. Sure, some have more value today while others don't, but at the end of the day, the value does not always only lie in the type of coin, as much as it lies in a variety of factors.

The Most Valuable U.S Coins

As you grow in this art, you are going to come across lots of coins in different denominations. Now, there are at least 7 U.S coins that are considered to be the most valuable in the numismatic world today. Every coin collector who is interested in American coins should be aware of these coins. Even if you are a total beginner and despite how you want to approach coin collecting, I believe that you should know these coins.

In case you come across them as you collect, their identity is as follows:

The 1794 Flowing Hair Dollar

It is believed that this coin was the first-ever silver dollar coin struck by a U.S mint. It was minted both in 1794 and 1795 and its silver content is 90%. Also, it is considered to be the finest coin of its time that is in existence today. In 2013, this coin fetched a whopping $10 million in an auction at Stack's Bowers Galleries. I can't tell you its exact value because it constantly changes year by year. There is also the 1974 flowing dollar, which is equally important, as it is the first coin dollar to be standardized across the country.

1870 S Seated Liberty Dollar

This is quite an intriguing coin because there is no official record of its existence. 11 traced specimens supposedly exist but there has not been an official confirmation that they are actually there. Among these dollars, the ones with an S min mark, an indication that they were minted in San Francisco are the most valuable ones. All of them have a percentage of silver equal to 90%. If you find one of these coins you will probably notice their bad conditions. It's almost impossible to find these coins in good conditions.

The 1913 Liberty Head Nickel

Only a very small quantity of these Nickels was produced by the United States mint. This means that it is a rare coin that is especially valuable to modern day coin collectors. It is reported that only five Liberty Head Nickels are known to be in existence today. Two of them are housed in museums and the other three are owned privately. Imagine if you found one. Yours would be the sixth. How amazing would that be!

The 1838 O Capped Bust Half Dollar

This coin is said to have come into existence during the time the New Orleans Mint was opened, it was the first U.S mint to strike silver coins. This coin is very rare making it to be extremely valuable to numismatics. It is commonly believed that only 20 of these coins were minted. Out of these, only nine have survived to be in existence today. Coin collecting experts do really appreciate not only its rarity but its design too. The representation of the eagle is considered one of the most well represented among all US coins. Not to mention its weight, which is 13.36 grams!

The 1927 D St. Gauden's Double Eagle

Former President of the United States Roosevelt recalled all the gold coins. Either in circulation or in bank vaults, they were converted to gold bars or melted completely. This happened in 1933. Among those gold coins was our 1917 D St. Gauden's Double Eagle. They were one of the lowest mintage coins of the Gauden's double series with the original minted number standing at 180, 000. It seems that a few people did not return these coins during the recall, as there are about 11 to 15 pieces still in existence today. They were very valuable then, as they are gold coins, but now, the rarity factor has made them even more valuable.

The 1776 Silver Continental Dollar

When America found freedom, almost right after the signing of the Declaration of Independence, the new United Congress wanted something to commemorate and mark their independence for the future. There was no better way to do this than strike the first true American currency. This coin had an outstanding design, which is attributed to the then-president Benjamin Franklin. It includes a whimsical motif and the words "fugio", which is interpreted as "times flies" as well as "mind your business". Also, there are 13 interlocking rings that represented the different colonies. A large number was struck but given the centuries that have passed since then, it is only normal that only a few can be traced. It needs to be mentioned that the silver version of these coins is almost extinct; it is very rare to find.

The 1867 Confederate States Half-Dollar

In 1861, the New Orleans mint was taken over by the confederate states. They did not have a reserve of precious metals to use in minting coins; therefore, they chose to use paper money other than coinage to support their war efforts. However, there were few confederate cents as well as half dollars that were struck. No one knew about them until they began showing up in the hands of private collectors post the civil war.

The Close "AM" Penny

Why would a space between A and M in America make a coin unique and valuable? This is because coins are minted very precisely and there should not be any mistakes. This is why any slight deviation from the precision catches the attention of collectors.

A deviation happens in 1992 when pennies were being minted (in Philadelphia). The spacing between the "A" and "M" in "United States of America" on the reverse of the penny was closer than usual thus the name "Close AM".

There are only five known pieces of 1992 P- in existence. There are also others minted in Denver 1992- D. 15 pieces have been located. One of them was sold for $20, 700 in 2012.

11 Valuable U.S Coins That Are Still in Circulation Today

The above coin types are extremely rare to find, as they are no longer available for circulation. You won't get them in your change in your supermarket. Most of them are sitting in museums for people to admire while others are resting in prestigious collectors' coin albums. This is not to say that you can't stumble upon one on an ancient site with your metal detector. It's good to have hope for good things, right?

Now, in case you never stumble on those ones, it does not mean that you will never have a valuable coin in your collection. There are valuable coins that are still in circulation today! Many commonly used coins are appraised at a much higher value when compared to their face value. You may not need to buy them. Actually, since they are still in circulation, you might find them in your coin jar.

Are you wondering what those valuable coins that may be in your coin jar or in your next change at the mall might be?

Well, look for the following:

The 1955 Double Die Penny

This is a unique coin featuring a double image because of a mis-alignment in the minting process. 20,000 of these coins were released for circulation in 1955, most of them being distributed as change. It has no mint mark and has a face value of $0.01. If you happen to have one that is in good condition today, it could sell for around $1,800.

The 1982 No Mint Mark Roosevelt Dime

In 1982, the Philadelphia Mint mistakenly omitted the letter "p" from the Roosevelt Dime. This means that this coin does not have a mintmark. It is not clear how many of these were distributed, but up to 10,000 have been recorded to be in existence. It has a face value of $0. 10, but in the numismatic world, it is estimated to be worth $300.

The 1943 Lincoln Head Copper Penny

This is a copper coin, which was minted at a time of war when copper was sorely needed for the war effort and was not being used to create coins. The copper penny collection was created accidentally. During this time, the most common pennies were made out of silver and coated with silver such that they had a shiny appearance. Very few of the copper coins left the mint during this period. This is why the Lincoln Head Copper Penny of 1943 is rare and could fetch up to $10,000.

The 1969 S Lincoln Cent With Double Die Obverse

This is a very special coin. It was the only one to be featured On Americas 'most wanted' list of the Federal Bureau of Investigation. Beware that there may be fake ones still circulating as this was one coin that counterfeiters Morton Goodman and Roy Gray produced very similar coins to these ones, thus attracting overwhelming attention from the authorities. It is reported that less than a hundred authentic pieces were produced. Because of its rarity, it attracts high prices. Actually, it has an estimated value of up to $126,000 in auctions.

The 2004 Wisconsin State Quarter With Extra Leaf

If you are a State Quarter fanatic, this coin may be a very interesting one to collect. 453 million of this Quarter were minted in 2004. Of these, several thousand somehow ended up with an extra leaf on a husk of corn on the tails side. It is said that a mint employee intentionally made this "mistake". The error is what makes this coin valuable to collectors. Considering the quality of the coin, 'extra leaf' quarters sell for up to $1499. About five thousand of Quarters have been found in Tucson. Therefore, if you live around this area, you may want to double-check your pocket change or your coin jar. You don't know, you might be one of the lucky owners of the Extra Leaf State Quarter.

The 2005 P "In God We Rust" State Quarter

This is an error coin. They should have written "In God We Trust" but a mistake was made at the mint and the "T" was omitted and instead, the word 'Rust' is what ended up on the coin instead of "Trust". The error was not intended to make any statement about government or religion—the explanation was that there was a buildup of grease in the coin die when filling T. This error coin is not that uncommon and thus it may not fetch much in the market. It has a face value of $0.25. However, some collectors find it pretty fascinating, as the mistake is quite in an interesting place. It can be sold for about $100.

The 1997 Double Ear Lincoln Penny

Abraham Lincoln may not have had the perfect or rather common features. He was uncommonly tall and had a facial asymmetry condition just to mention a few of his abnormalities. However, he never had double ear lobes, but there is an error coin with a portrait of him that indicates this. It was minted in 1997 and is commonly known as the Double Ear Lincoln penny. It is that "the double ear" feature that makes the coin valuable in the collectors' world and it can sell for up to $250.

The 2005 Speared Bison Jefferson Nickel

On the back of this Nickel is a buffalo that appears to be pierced from underneath. This is an error that occurred when the die got a scratch at the time of minting the coin. It makes a beautiful detail on the coin. However, this coin is not considered to be very valuable; it has a face value of $0.5 but there was an exception. It is reported that a 2005-D 5C Speared Bison Jefferson Nickel was sold for up to $ 1,265 at an auction.

The 1999 P Broad Struck Quarter

This is another Quarter that has turned out to have more value than its face value due to an error made during the minting process; its face value is $0.25 but it has an estimated value of $25. What is the error? The coin was "broad struck" which means that it was not properly lined up with the machine when it was struck. It seems to have an "over growth" on a part of the edge which gives it quite an "abnormal" appearance. Have you noticed that? Sometimes errors are difficult to spot and it can be challenging to notice them.

The 2007 "Godless" Presidential Dollar Coin

Every U.S currency has the infamous "In God We Trust" inscription, but apparently not all of them did, at least not in 2007. In that year, the new George Washington one-dollar coins were released in the U.S. It is said that an unknown number of them, were not inscribed with the infamous 'logo' accidentally. Out here, they are termed "Godless", but the official name for them is "Missing Edge Lettering" dollars. Tens of thousands of these coins have been found and their price lies between $29 and $228.

The Roosevelt Silver Dimes and Washington Silver Quarters

Modern day dimes and quarters are made from copper and nickel alloys; there is no trace of silver. However, before 1965, at least 95% of their composition was silver. These coins are not rare but they still sell for more than their face value because of the silver metal composition.

COIN COLLECTING FOR BEGINNERS

CHAPTER 3

WHERE DO I GET MY COINS?

Coin collecting has begun just as a pastime for many people. Nevertheless, you can hear other individuals state (or you most likely have heard them yourselves) about the stories of individuals earning money with their old coins. That inspired more individuals to go on a coin-collecting journey. If you are among those individuals who wish to buy coins, there are numerous locations to begin your collection.

Coin Shops

A few store owners are dealers who understand a great deal about the coins and are selling certain coins. These coin stores are an important location to discover and find out more about coin collecting and coins. These coin stores could be expensive as they are seeking to sell their coins for a profit. With adequate understanding and having somebody who understands a lot about coin collecting by you, you can get terrific prices.

I personally discourage people to buy from coin shops if they are total beginners because you risk to pay much more than the real value of a coin. In addition, many owners are not very open to negotiating the price and most of the time or you buy at their price or you leave. However, if you are a total newbie, I encourage you to visit them without buying to know more about coins and how they are graded.

Coin Shows

There are times when your neighborhood mall will have a display from several coin dealers. These will allow you to see their collection and enable you to get a few of them for a lower price because of competitors. You will most likely see many brand-new coins that are up for grabs and great for your collection.

These coin shows are fantastic, not just for collectors. But also, for coin lovers who wish to see uncommon and difficult-to-find coins.

The first time it's always better to go with someone more expert than you, but even if you are a beginner as you probably are, you can find good deals and people that are open to telling you interesting and unique stories about coins.

The main drawback of coin shows is that they are not run in any town or city. If you reside in a small city or town you might need to drive to the next big city.

Mail Orders/Web Sites

There are countless dealers worldwide, and most of them have sites that enable you to pay them via mail order or any internet payment system like PayPal. You ought to conduct your research on these businesses and read their terms thoroughly to ascertain you can get your cash back when you have issues with the coin you got.

There are most likely numerous phony websites that are simply aiming to get your cash for one genuine website. You ought to ask for some feedback and lots of images before paying anyone online and keep in mind not to release any PINs or passwords.

Sadly, more and more coin-related fraud has been taking place online in recent years. Check for the best deals, but pay attention to the details. You don't want to be the next one to be scammed.

Flea Markets

This sort of location is an unexpected place to find uncommon coins. Nevertheless, these locations have various notions of prices, so because of their absence of understanding of coin pricing. You will discover pricey coins; however, if you are fortunate, you may discover an uncommon coin someplace in those stacks of coins, which will make it worth your time.

Flea market sellers typically search for a fast sale and would most likely offer you discounts when you purchase their products in bulk. Try to purchase other products and get your coin included as a reward. I know it might sound weird but trust me, sometimes even if you are new to coin collecting you know more about the seller!

Auctions

If you want to invest in uncommon coins, the ideal location to go would be in an auction. Auctions are the only locations where you may discover individuals selling their rarest and most pricey coins.

Many of these auctions are occurring on the web, and most sellers are searching for the best bidders. Nevertheless, you need to be cautioned that a few of these sellers are scams and will not make the price you pay rewarding. You ought to attempt to find out more about these coins and their value before purchasing one from an online auction.

Other Coin Collectors

Coin collectors generally have replicated coins to sell for a lower price than their market price. The only issue is that it is difficult to discover another coin collector like you. The very best locations to look at are forums, online groups, and neighborhood groups. Other coin collectors are the ideal individuals to go to when you wish to begin your collection. They can provide you with suggestions, discount rates, and you may even entice some to provide you with a few of their coins to kick-start your collection. You might be surprised to discover how supportive the coin collecting community is. When I first started my coin collection, I was given three coins by another coin collector, and for free!

CHAPTER 4

PROTECT YOUR COLLECTION

A cardinal rule for all coin collectors is to avoid causing wear or introducing any substances that may cause spots or color changes. Try to avoid any direct manual contact with your coins. This means not using your bare hands to handle the coins. Fingerprints are collectible coin's sworn enemies. It is also fundamental to ensure that you do not let one coin touch another coin because it can result in nicks and scratches. To avoid ruining them, remove coins from their storage containers only when needed and necessary. Please, note that showing a coin to your friend is not considered necessary!

Uncirculated or Proof coins should not be handled anywhere but the edge, as even a slight fingerprint may reduce its grade and, consequently its value. Proof coins are those struck two or more times with polished dyes on an equally polished planchet; they are legal tender like any regular coins. Uncirculated mint sets are coins packaged by the US government for sale to coin collectors. It is best if you make it a habit to pick up collectible coins by their edges while wearing clean white cotton or surgical gloves. A face mask is also preferable to prevent small particles of moisture that may cause unwanted spots. Never sneeze or cough near coins because this can leave marks and ruin the coin. If you are thinking that these precautions are too exaggerated and that you don't need them, prepare to see your coin collection ruined by time without you even noticing that. I sadly know some coin collectors that underestimated the impact of external factors on their coins and they now have a ruined coin collection.

Mint Coins

Coin holders provide enough protection for ordinary handling. If you must take the coin out and need to put it down outside the holder, make sure you place it on a clean and soft surface, preferably a velvet pad.

It is an ideal surface and a must-have for handling valuable numismatic materials.

For coins with lesser value, clean, soft cloth may be used. Avoid dragging coins on any surface to avoid scratches. Take note that even wiping with a soft cloth can cause scratches that will reduce its value.

Coin Care and Cleaning

While it is good to maintain cleanliness in the surroundings, it is best not to clean the coins. A shiny coin may look nice, but maintaining its original appearance is essential for a collectible coin.

Cleaning the coin can reduce its numismatic value significantly. There are only a very restricted number of things you can do to improve the appearance of a coin. You might harm it instead of enhancing it.

Unnecessary cleaning affects the value and cost of collectible coins. The patina on a coin is built up over the years and is part of its total essence and history and reflects a value much more than its face value. Eliminate it, and you can lessen its worth by as much as 90%! Hoarders price coins by means of good-looking patinas, which, in effect, shield the coin's surface.

Like any work of art restoration, cleaning coins must be done by professionals. They know what techniques to employ that will work best and still have the coin as valuable as ever.

If you think that a tarnished coin you have just revealed needs to be cleaned, STOP! It is not a good idea. It is better to leave the coin as it is now. The color change you observe is a natural process called toning. And if allowed to progress by itself naturally and produce attractive results, it sometimes adds to the coin's value.

Toning is caused by the atoms' chemical reactions on the coin's surface, usually with sulfur compounds. It cannot be reversed, but "dips" in which strip molecules from the coin's surface are available. Bear in mind, however, that professionals should only do this.

You need to observe several rules when considering cleaning the coins you have obtained, found, bought, or inherited.

Never clean a coin that you do not know the numismatic value. If you doubt if it's valuable or not, then don't clean it either. It is best to leave coins the way you found them, untouched. Erring on the conservative side is preferable to ruining the coin for nothing. Store them in holders made for the purpose. Coin collectors and dealers prefer coins in their original condition, so do not attempt to alter their state. Cleaning will probably ensure more harm than good.

Because you are not supposed to clean the coins yourself, you need to take the coins to a professional coin cleaning service. Most of them use a technique called "dipping" that will properly clean the coins without reducing their value. This is important, especially if the coin's date and details cannot be determined because of corrosion. A professional will be knowledgeable on how to avoid or minimize further damage to the coin.

In the situation that you must clean a coin, you have found, then do it with the least harmful method. Do not use harsh chemicals, sulfuric acid, polishing cloth, vinegar, abrasive pastes, or devices that give a smooth and shiny result on the coin. Experiment first with lesser value coins before coins with high value.

Cleaning is a big issue in coin collecting, so you have to disclose this fact to a buyer if you are selling a coin that you know has been cleaned.

Cleaning Different Types of Coins

Despite we have just touched on the basic rules you need to keep in mind when cleaning coins, you can find below a list of a series of cleaning tips you should keep in mind related to specific coins.

- **Uncirculated coins:** they should never be cleaned at all because cleaning will ruin any mint luster.
- **Gold Coins:** they should be cleansed cautiously in neat, lukewarm bubbly purified liquid consuming a cottony fiber wash-down fabric or an incredibly easy tooth scrub. Gold is smooth metal, so you should take extra care to avoid disfiguring or scratching.
- **Silver Coins:** valuable silver coins should not be cleaned at all. The blue-green or violet oil-like tarnish, dirt, minerals, or other residues some silver coins have enhances their appearance and should be left alone. Dark silver coins must be cleaned with ammonia, rubbing alcohol, vinegar, or polish remover with acetone. Do not rub or polish them.
- **Copper Coins:** if necessary to clean, soak copper coins in grape oil. If not available, olive oil will do. Never attempt to rub them in any way. However, getting results may take time, from several weeks to a year, so be patient.
- **Nickel Coins:** these coins are best cleaned with warm, soapy distilled water using a soft toothbrush. If cleaning badly stained nickel coins, use ammonia diluted 3 to 1 with distilled water.

How to Store Your Coins

You need to store your coins properly to avoid giving them any scratch to reduce their numismatic value. You need to use the right kind of holder, depending on the value of the coin you are storing.

There are folders and albums available commercially that you can purchase for storing your series or type collection. When using paper envelopes, make sure that their materials are especially suited for holding coins, especially the high-value ones, since sulfur or other chemicals present in the paper can cause a reaction and change the coin's color.

Plastic flips made of mylar and acetate are good materials for long-term storage, but since they are hard and brittle, they may scratch the coin if they are not inserted and removed carefully. "Soft" flips used to be created after polyvinyl chloride (PVC), which decayed after some time and imparted grievous ends aimed at the coinages. The PVC gave the pennies an emerald look. PVC reverses are certainly no longer manufactured and marketed in the US.

Tubes can hold several same-size coins and are seemingly for the majority space of distributed coinages and higher-grade coins if they are not moved. For more valuable coins, use hard plastic holders as they do not contain harmful materials and can protect coins against scratches and other physical damage.

Collectible Coins in Their Cases

For more valuable coins, you can opt to use slabs as they offer good protection. Slabs are hermetically sealed hard plastic holders for individual coins. However, one drawback is the expense involved, and you will not be able to get at the coin easily if there is a need to do so.

For long-term storage, a dry environment without significant temperature fluctuation and low humidity are important. You need to minimize exposure to moist air, as this will cause oxidation. It may not reduce the coin's value but reducing oxidation will help the coin look more attractive. To control atmospheric moisture, you need to place silica gel packets in the coin storage area.

You still need to check on your collection periodically, even if you store them in a safety deposit box. If not stored properly, problems could develop, and you can do something about it before any serious damage occurs.

Protecting Your Collection From Loss by Fire or Theft

There will always be the threat of loss by fire or theft to any of your properties. However, just as you would protect your house or car from them, there are some precautions you can take to minimize them. Bear in mind that most homeowner insurance excludes coins and other items of numismatic value from coverage. You can usually get a rider, however, but for an additional premium payment.

You can also obtain a separate policy. Consider joining the American Numismatic Association (ANA), which offers insurance for its members' coin collections. Make sure you have a catalog of your collection stored separately from the coins. Note where you have obtained each coin, the condition of the coin, and the price you paid for it.

Taking individual close-up pictures of each coin is also a good idea. Get an appraisal from a professional who uses a Blue Book or Red Book for this purpose. The insurance company will need the documents for the appraisal.

Safes protect against theft, fire, dust, water, or other environmental factors that could damage your possessions. For your coins, they offer relative protection. Some safes provide adequate protection from fire but are not suitable for theft protection.

Some safes do deter thieves but are not fireproof. Your collection can be damaged or destroyed by fire even if the flames do not touch your coins. The heat may be extreme enough to melt them.

Another concern when storing your coins in a safe is the level of humidity. A high level will cause oxidation, which is bad for the coins. The ideal level is 30% relative humidity (RH). The RH inside the safe is dependent on the ambient RH where the safe is located. Most modern safes, fortunately, are adequately insulated and are constructed with good seals. Silica gel packets can help reduce humidity.

So, if you opt to keep your collection at home, see that you get a home safe that provides enough fire and humidity protection and protection against theft. Make sure you take measures to prevent or dissuade a burglar from invading your home. Adequate lighting and secure, strong locks are recommended. You can ask law enforcement officers for more valuable tips.

One way of protecting your investment against theft is to be discrete about being a coin collector. The information you divulge about yourself with many people may eventually reach the wrong person. Having all numismatic-related promotional materials sent to a post office box instead of your home may help.

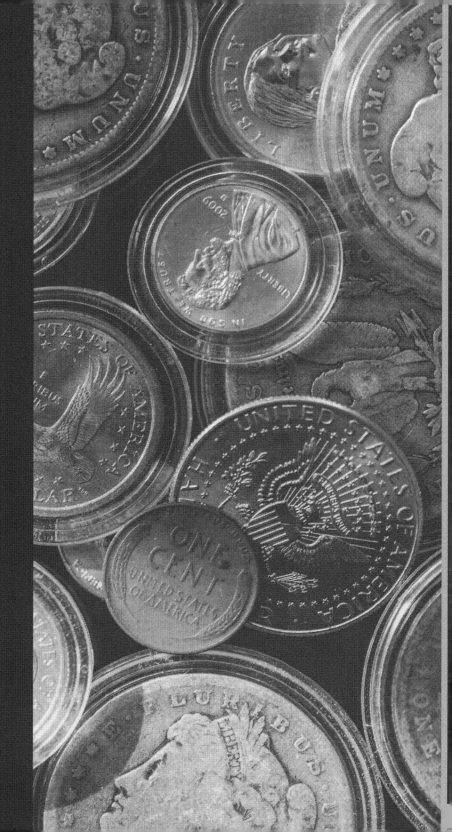

COIN COLLECTING FOR BEGINNERS

CHAPTER 5

BRITISH AND WORLDWIDE COINS

W hen someone uses the term world coins, most people think of coins produced during the past 100 years or so. People are always impressed with any coin dating from the 1800s. Yet coins go back thousands of years. Even modern coins typically encompass issues of the past 500 years. There is a lot out there to be collected.

British Coins

British coins are an important part of British culture and history, but it can be a bit confusing to collect when you're just starting out. This breaks down the various types of British coins to help collectors find what interests them, as well as make it easier for them to learn more about these valuable pieces of history.

There are many different types of British coins, and they were issued in various denominations. Coins from around this time were usually made of precious metal or base metal depending on their value in terms of their weight. For example, half-sovereigns were made out of silver, but sovereigns were made out of gold. Although the British half-sovereign had a more "official" name, it was also referred to as a sovereign in everyday conversation.

British coinage changed over time with many different additions and subtraction of coins. Each type has its own history and significance to the British government that you'll need to learn about before buying these coins.

There are several types of collectors that enjoy collecting these coins. These collectors include those that are interested in collecting Queen Elizabeth's coinage or those who are interested in the coinage of a specific monarch. There are also some people who enjoy collecting by "periods". This means they focus on finding certain types of coins that were made during one specific period of time. For instance, you could collect from about 1750 to 1850 if you're just looking to collect from the colonial period of Great Britain. Other important periods include Roman Britannia, Medieval and Viking coins as well as coins from the early Norman Kings.

A final type of collector will collect two coins from each year since they were first minted. This can be a fun way to assemble a collection that is very easy to display and also easy to keep track of.

There are many different types of British coins that are worth collecting and some are worth much more than others. All British coins have specific mintmarks that tell you where the coin was minted, so this can help you identify which coin is more valuable if there's any difference in value. For instance, coins from the London mint, which was near the Tower of London are usually more valuable than those minted in other locations.

Let's take a look at some good coins to collect and the price range they're likely to sell for. You can also use these lists to help you determine how long it should take you to complete your collection. How many British coins do you have? Are there any missing? Take the time to check some of the more popular ones that could cost tens of thousands of dollars.

The list below includes the most iconic British coins of all times with an explanation of their value in today's money.

Half Sovereigns

Half sovereigns were minted from 1661 to 1816 and then from 1928 to 1948. With the end of the Gold Standard, this coin has been produced only in very small quantities. Although, this coin is still legal tender. This coin today would be worth at least $1,500 in today's money and around $10,000 for a red one.

Sovereigns

Sovereigns were minted in 1787 and 1817 with the exception of the year 1793 when they were minted in the Netherlands. Half sovereigns were also made in 1787 and 1817 as well. The production of sovereigns stopped with the beginning of the First World War because it was replaced by paper money. Both of these coins would sell for at least $2,000 today if they're gold-colored or more if they're silver-colored.

Two-Shilling

Two-shilling coins were made from 1797 to 1836. Curious to know is that these coins have been introduced as part of an experiment about decimalization that was interrupted. These are some of the most valuable British coins since there are so few of them, and they can sell for as much as $25,000.

Shield Pennies

Shield pennies were issued from 1684 to 1756 with the exception of 1689 when no pennies were issued. These coins weren't reissued again until 1929 when they were worth one penny; however, they weren't minted again until 1948. A lot of these Shield pennies could be found in circulation today and would be worth about $100 in today's money if you found one at an antique show or coin shop.

Copper Halfpennies

Copper Halfpennies were minted between 1797 and 1821. The last ones were made in 1821 until they were discontinued and not re-adopted until 1928 in brassy colors. These coins are worth at least $1,000 in today's money and around $3,000 for a red example. If you decide to collect British coins this coin is probably the one from which you should start your collection. Not too rare but certainly valuable.

Three pence

Three pences were minted from 1560 to 1931, when the last coins were made in 1931 until they were discontinued. This coin is most known because other countries adopted the name for their national coins. These countries are Australia, New Zealand and South Africa. These coins have a value of at least $200 in today's money and are appealing to collectors because they're so rare. I personally consider these coins one of the most fascinating among all the British coins.

Sixpence

Sixpences were minted from 1670 to 1889, when the last coins were issued in 1889 until they were discontinued, making this series one of the rarest and most valuable coins in British history. If you visit a coin shop specialized in British coins you might hear the owner calling this coin "tanner". This is the name originally given to this coin. The king represented in the coin is Edward VI.

Pennies

Pennies were minted since they started being issued in 1489 until 1971 when the last pennies were made until today. The value of these alloys is determined by their surface quality and individual condition, which might bring them up to about $50 to $100 in today's money. This is by far the easiest coin to find even if you are in the US. However, most of them are not worth a lot so you will need to look for the rarest editions.

Medieval Versus Early Modern

Machine-produced coins were introduced into different countries at different times in history. For this reason, machine-struck coins of England, for example, appear significantly earlier than do machine-struck coins in Russia. It isn't difficult to identify one method of manufacture from another. Just examine the fabric and appearance of the individual coins.

In most parts of Europe, the economy was predominantly agrarian from approximately the fall of the Roman Empire until the Renaissance. As the Renaissance advanced and the modern European economy went from barter to money, the need for coins also increased dramatically.

Silver mining in such places as Bohemia became increasingly important as did the demand for higher denomination coins in significant numbers. The discovery of gold and silver in the Americas became just as important. So did the need to be able to produce coins from the metals being mined not only in larger numbers, but of sufficiently consistent purity, weight, design, and diameter. Modern machinery could fill this need.

The Early Modern Era

Medieval coins are generally defined as coins produced completely by hand, whereas early modern coins are those coins produced using hand-operated machinery. The method of manufacture determines the period into which the coin fits.

European Coins

England began to use milled coinage in 1662. The country used the pound system, which consisted of a mix of pence, shillings, florins, pounds, and crowns. This continued until a decimalized monetary system was introduced during the 1970s.

The Netherlands began its modern coinage in 1586 when the Earl of Leicester as governor-general of the Netherlands limited the number of mints in operation to one mint for each province. In 1602, the States-General introduced a uniform system of denominations and coin types. The Congress of Vienna established the Kingdom of the Netherlands in 1815. The Netherlands joined the European Union currency union in 2002.

France began using the centime-franc coinage system during the sixteenth century, the system was established by the kings of Valois. The mint in Paris began using machines to strike coins by 1640 during the reign of Louis XIV. Magnificent gold and silver coins followed. Decimal coinage was introduced in the 1790s during the French Revolution, and France adopted the euro in 2002.

Italy and Germany are fascinating areas to collect, as each was divided into states until the late nineteenth century, and many of these states issued their own coins. Despite the diversity of issues, the system was not chaotic, since each coin-issuing entity made the denominations, weight, and purity of their coins consistent with those of other states.

In 2001, the euro currency system replaced the coins and banknotes of twelve European Union countries. This is the largest currency union in history.

Spain became a unified nation in 1492. Its coinage system, based on the gold 8-escudos and 8-real coins, is remembered today because the coins were cut into pie-piece shaped "pieces of eight" to make a change. Spain's coinage system was also used by its vast Spanish colonial American system of mints. The system survived through the Napoleonic invasions, but during the late nineteenth century, it was replaced with the more modern decimal peseta-based coinage system. This system was continued through the dictatorship of Francisco Franco during the mid-twentieth century and beyond, but it was finally retired in favor of the euro in 2002.

Russian coinage was modernized during the reign of Czar Peter the Great, who ruled between 1689 and 1725. In 1711, machine-struck coins were first produced at the newly constructed Moscow mint. In 1719, the mint and its machinery were moved to St. Petersburg. Czarist Russian coinage continued through 1917, with Soviet coins and notes being issued through the early 1990s, this, in turn, was followed by the coins and banknotes of the newly independent modern states that include Russia and the many breakaway states that were formerly parts of Soviet Europe and Asia.

Islamic Coins

Islamic coinage, just like any other coinage, is complex. There are common coins and there are rare coins. The many Islamic coin-issuing entities produced minor denomination coins in copper or bronze, with higher denomination dirhems in silver and dinars in gold. During what in Europe would have been the Middle Ages, gold rather than silver was the primary coinage metal driving the economy of the Islamic world. Unlike the mostly fractionalized nations of Europe, the Islamic caliphates of this period were united and flourished. Due to Islamic laws forbidding images, few coins depict anything other than an Islamic slogan.

Many collectors are squeamish about collecting Islamic coins because they are unfamiliar with the Arabic script and calligraphy typically appearing on these coins, and disappointed by the lack of any iconography other than this artistic script appearing on most issues.

You can identify these Arabic legends or slogans with several specialized coin books on the subject. Most of these coins are simple to read with the assistance of such a reference. The price of even the gold dinar and silver dirhem denominated coins is typically reasonable when compared to U.S. and modern world coin prices.

Chinese Coins

The coinage history of China is similar to that of Islam; there is no true medieval period for their coinage. In 1861, round silver dollar, or yuan, coins were issued in Fukien Province. Two years later, Hong Kong, already under British control, opened its own mint to strike European-style coins. In 1889, imperial China's first modern mint opened in Canton. The yuan or dollar was declared to be the central coin of the economy in 1910.

China's modern period begins at this point. Some of the most desirable Chinese coins from this period are the Communist Army issues of the civil war period of the 1930s. Even many of the low denomination coins are rare. Coinage of the Peoples' Republic of China begins in 1955. Although today China issues precious metal "Panda" coins, it wasn't until 2004 that it became legal for Chinese citizens to own gold.

Coinage in the Americas

The indigenous people of North America used barter rather than coins until the time European traders and settlers introduced money as we know it. The greatest impact came from the early settlers who established New Spain, New France, New Netherlands, New Sweden, and New England. Each of these colonies and its governing authority in Europe vied for supremacy over this new world, with Great Britain eventually coming to dominate North America.

New Spain

New Spain actually included part of North America (Mexico) as well as Central and South America with the exception of Portuguese Brazil. At least one very rare token is known that can be linked to Florida, but most of the Spanish colonial American coin issues were struck at mints scattered about their possessions in Mexico and points south.

The primary mission of the Spanish colonial American mints was to strike as many gold and silver coins as was physically possible, shipping most of them back to Spain where the treasure ships in which they were loaded were typically impounded by local bankers owed money by the Spanish crown to finance the monarchy's costly wars in Europe.

Initially, the coins were made by rolling the gold or silver into a cylinder of precious metal from which the coinage blanks were cut just as a disk could be cut from a corncob. For this reason, these barbarically made coins were called cobs. The machine struck coinage followed, using a collar to make the coins round. Machine techniques ensured better quality coins, with more consistent weight as well.

Spanish colonial American coins can be collected by denomination and date; however, the mint mark and the initials of the mint master also appear in the legends on the reverse. These mintmarks and initials are important since some are rarer than others.

You can use a good foreign coin book to identify the many mintmarks appearing on Spanish colonial American coins. In general, the most common coins carry the Mexico City mint mark (a small O resting on a larger M).

The Spanish colonial period ended during the early nineteenth century, varying from country to country depending on when the local revolutions succeeded. The awkward Spanish system based on the gold 8-escudos and silver 8-real coins was soon replaced with decimal coinage systems that are still in place today.

Most of the coinage struck for New Spain was produced in Central and South America due to the abundant gold and silver mines throughout that region. Many of these coins circulated in North America during the colonial period simply because there were few coins being imported into the North American colonies from elsewhere. It wasn't until 1857 that it became illegal for foreign precious metals (gold and silver) or specie coins to circulate as currency in the United States. A majority of these foreign coins were struck at mints somewhere in New Spain.

You can collect Spanish colonial American coins by denomination, date, and mint mark in a similar manner to collecting coins of the United States. Some are rare, while others are not. In general, the most common Spanish colonial American coins are those struck in Mexico City. The mint mark for this mint is a large M on which rests a small O.

Spanish colonial American silver coins were struck in 8-, 4-, 2-, 1-, and half-real denominations, with gold coins struck in 8-, 4-, 2-, 1-, and half escudo denominations. The smaller denominations are "pieces of eight."

New France

The Company of the Hundred Associates was organized to colonize New France in 1627. Montreal was founded in 1642 followed by the founding of Louisiana in 1699. The Gloriam Regni coinage produced for all French overseas colonies in 1670 was shipped to Acadia and Canada the same year. A chronic shortage of coins for Canada and other French territories led to the countermarking of Spanish coins with a fleur de lis for local circulation. In 1685 playing cards were specially marked as currency to pay French military troops stationed in Canada, but these proved to be unpopular.

France continued to make coins for its colonies. Louis XV ordered 6- and 12-denier copper coins for the colonies in 1716, while a denier copper coin was sent to New France under his authorization in 1721. Four years later, the ship Le Chameau sank off Cape Breton Island on its way to Quebec and Louisbourg, loaded with gold and silver coins.

France ceded Canada to England in 1763. In the ensuing years, privately issued and banker tokens were produced and circulated throughout Canada. In 1858, the first federal issues were minted.

Canada's colonial coinage period ends in 1857. Its large cents were introduced in 1858 just as the United States ceased issuing theirs. Canada introduced its silver dollar in 1935, the year the U.S. ceased producing its silver dollar.

Today Canada has a decimal system of coins and banknotes similar to those used in the United States. Collectors tend to either collect Canadian coins by denomination, date, and mintmark, or they collect colonial issues. Collectors in Canada refer to their modern coinage as "decimals."

Modern World Coins

Ancient coins are sometimes considered synonymous with gold or silver coins. However, this might not always be the case, as other materials were also used to make coins in ancient times (such as glass, ivory, or porcelain, for example).

What about modern world coins?

There are almost a countless number of modern world coins to be collected. Collectors can choose between coins meant to circulate as money, precious metal coins meant to trade as bullion, and the many commemorative coins struck by mints for the benefit of governments' coffers.

Some people collect coins from a specific country, others collect for a specific theme that appears on the coins regardless of their origin, and still others choose the daunting task of collecting a single coin from every coin issuer in the world. Ways to collect are limited only by your imagination and creativity.

Evolution of the Use of Coins

One of the more important events in modern world coin history occurred in 1484. That's when the Archduke Sigismund of Austria (in Tyrol) declared that the value of 60 kreuzers in silver coins would be known as the gulden groschen, in turn, this gulden groschen was valued at one gold florin. In 1520, Count Stephen Schlik and his brother struck large diameter silver coins at Joachimstal in Bohemia. The coins were soon known as the Joachimstaler, then as the thaler, taler, dalder, dollar, and other similar names. Large-denomination coins were taking center stage.

Modern technology slowly replaced the old-fashioned way of making coins by hand. Steam presses eventually replaced humans and horse power. As European monarchs began to gain better control of their countries, these monarchs centralized their power. During the Middle Ages, it had been common for local mints to be in operation throughout the realm for the convenience of coinage distribution.

This centralization of power also led to centralized coinage production as well. The number of mints in most countries began to decrease as they developed centralized minting facilities.

As the modern economic world dawned, coinage was in regular use primarily throughout Europe, Asia, and the Americas. Australia and Africa followed once these two became viable modern economic regions. Coinage in India, just as in Italy and Germany, was eventually centralized as was the government.

Modern Innovations

The first truly modern innovation in coinage was modern machinery and modern energy methods to run those machines. This was followed by a reduction machine, which made identical working coinage dies of the appropriate size from a master coin design model.

Dates and mintmarks became commonplace on coins. Most countries began using Christian calendar dates, but even today there are countries that do not.

As technology improved, so did the metals that could be used to make coins. Nickel, aluminum, and many different alloys were employed. Some of these metals proved to be more durable than their precious metal predecessors. In 1933, the gold standard for coins was abandoned, and during the 1960s the silver standard was abandoned worldwide.

Today, mintage in circulation is no longer based on the intrinsic value of each coin. Faith in the government and the local economy is why we accept modern coins as money.

Modern technology also allowed circulating coins to vary in shape. Scallops, six-sided and even eight-sided coins were produced. The edge of coins is sometimes reeded, other times appears with a lettered legend, while other times may appear as an interrupted combined reeded and plain edge.

Braille appears on some modern coins. Holographs have been developed for security purposes. Ringed bimetal coinage was made popular after its introduction in 1981 by the Italian state mint.

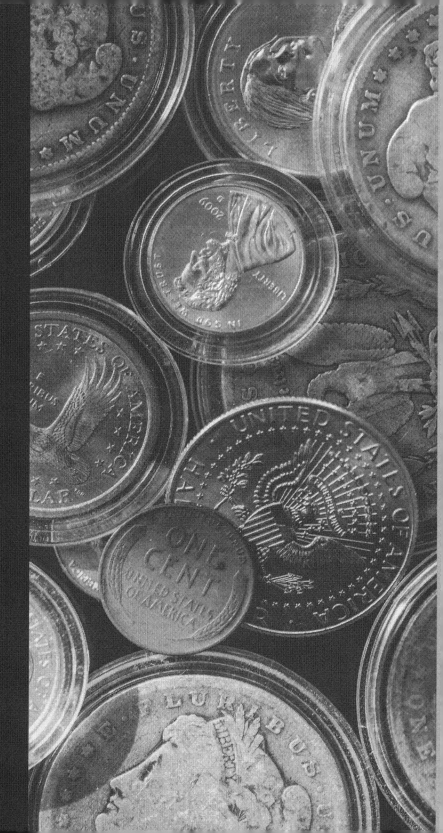

COIN COLLECTING FOR BEGINNERS

CHAPTER 6

MAKING MONEY WITH MONEY

Before we dive into the best techniques for selling your coins and making a profit for them, it's essential that you understand what makes a coin valuable and what features you should consider. Let's start!

What Makes Coins Valuable?

To make money with coins the most important thing that you need to understand is that it's a "buy and hold" type of investment. This means that you first buy a coin at the lowest possible price and you then sell it later for a higher price. The difference is your profit (if you decide to sell online you will also need to consider a commission taken by the platform).

Consequently, you need to apply the first rule of marketing, which consists of finding a market. In other words, you want to buy a coin today that you will be able to sell tomorrow. For this, you need a demand or, if you prefer, a general and consistent interest towards that specific coin. Spotting a coin that is in high demand can be very tricky but the two key things that you need to analyze are the following:

- The main characteristics of a coin (so, what a collector would generally look after)
- the main types of collectors (which might show different ranges of interest in different types of coins)

Once all this is cleared up, we will proceed with the main features that make coins generally valuable.

Coin Characteristics to Consider

Depending on the kind of coin collector you are, you might want to look after one or more of the following coin characteristics when considering whether or not to buy them:

- **Denomination:** Every currency puts out different denominations (such as the penny, the nickel, the dime, and the quarter, for example). If you want to go big, you could start collecting denominations that are obsolete as well (such as the 20-cent coin, for example).
- **Type:** This does not necessarily refer to the type of coins, but to the designs available for each denomination. For instance, a half dollar could be a Flowing Hair, a Franklin head, a Seated Liberty, a Walking Liberty, and so on.
- **Date:** Some people collect coins by the date they were issued, and that is perfectly fine. For instance, you might want to collect all types of nickels that were issued from 1900 to the current date (and you can also choose to skip the very rare and expensive ones if that is what you want).
- **Date and mintmark combination:** You might also want to collect coins according to the date and mintmark. Do keep in mind that this can be more expensive than just collecting them according to their date because most coin series have a particular mintmark that is very pricey. This is not true for all types of coins (in the sense described in the second bullet point in this list). For instance, collecting all the Barber dimes might get prohibitively expensive (as the rare ones can cost as much as $1,000,000). However, collecting all the Barber half-dollar coins might be affordable.
- **Year:** This type of collection includes all the coins issued in the year of your birth. If you are under 50 years old, doing this will be quite easy as you can just buy Mint sets. However, you might also want to set a different challenge (such as collecting

all coins released in another year of significance for you or for history in general).

Now, I realize all this could be a little confusing when you are just starting out your coin collection, but don't worry: as long as you are curious and read as much as you can on the topic, you will definitely get all the ins and outs of this lucrative hobby.

Where and How to Sell Your Coins

Just as with buying coins, there are many different platforms where you can sell your coins to make a profit. Whether you decide to sell online or to a dealer in person largely depends on your level of comfort with the internet, but as a general rule selling online will yield you more money.

If you'd prefer to not sell online, your best bet is to sell to a coin shop. My recommendation is to pick out the highest-rated coin shops in your area and bring your coins to the owners for a quote. Get quotes from multiple shops before committing to a deal so that you can maximize your selling price.

You can even call ahead to the coin shop to get a quote over the phone if what you're selling is relatively common or low-value. Keep in mind that a dealer will typically not have the time or inclination to go through a massive collection of Wheat cents (or whatever else) and evaluate each coin, so make sure to do an initial appraisal of your own and split out the highest-value coins from the rest of the pile.

If you have higher-value or rarer coins, it may be worth looking up the calendar of local coin shows in your area, dealers at coin shows often specialize in certain types of coins, and may be able to pay more money for coins within their area of specialization. Coin shop owners, on the other hand, are forced to be generalists and may not be able to offer as much money for niche selection.

If selling online, your options are more plentiful. eBay is always my primary recommendation, as it's relatively accessible and easy to use, and has a huge market of coin buyers. I'll go over some more specific recommendations for how to list and sell coins on eBay.

eBay is typically a strong market for coins under about $1000. If you have more premium material, you may instead want to consign your coins to a premium auction site.

Three of the larger premium auction sites are GreatCollections, David Lawrence Rare Coins, and Heritage Auctions. All three mainly sell U.S. coins, with smaller segments for world and ancient coins.

GreatCollections has no minimum consignment, but requires that all coins be slabbed and authenticated by the third-party grading companies NGC, PCGS, or ANACS. They charge a seller's consignment fee of 5% for coins that sell for less than $1000, and 0% for coins that sell for more than $1000. GreatCollections is my personal favorite as they have a skilled photographer on staff that does a great job in taking high-quality photos of each coin. Don't forget that the quality of the photo plays a big role in how much a coin sells for online.

David Lawrence Rare Coins (AKA "DLRC") has a minimum consignment value of $2500, meaning that they will only accept your consignment if you're consigning at least $2500 worth of coins with them. They also have a 15% consignment fee on all coins. DLRC has quite an avid following, and an especially strong market for early U.S. coins (18th and early 19th century). Their photos are terrible and look like they were produced with a scanner, which is why I generally avoid working with them.

Heritage Auctions is the biggest auction house of the three, and has a catalog that extends beyond coins to sports memorabilia and other rare collectibles. Heritage has a minimum consignment value of $5000, and a consignment fee of 15% (which can be negotiated down, depending on what you have). Heritage gets the most traffic out of the three due to its great marketing campaigns. The quality of its photos is somewhat inconsistent, but seems to have improved recently.

Beyond the auction sites, you can also sell directly to online dealers. PCGS has a great list of coin dealers and their specialties, so you can find a dealer who might be interested in buying whatever specific types of coins you have.

How to Sell Coins on eBay

This is a meaty topic, and could easily be turned into an eBook of its own. As an eBay Power Seller for over a decade, I've learned quite a bit about how best to maximize value when selling coins. But I'll try to condense down my advice as much as possible into the essentials.

Feedback Rating

Feedback score goes a long way on eBay. If you're entirely new to the website, you'll have zero feedback. That's a red flag for buyers, as it shows that you have no history of successfully completed transactions.

It may seem like a Catch-22, as the only way you'll be able to sell is by getting feedback, and the only way you can get feedback is by selling. But there are a couple of ways around it.

The easiest method is to simply buy things. You can earn feedback on eBay by buying or selling, so if you use eBay for a few of those everyday purchases you'd otherwise get off Amazon or somewhere else, you can quickly build up a solid feedback score.

The other option is to sell low-value coins at low prices. You won't get full value for your coins, as some buyers will be scared away by your low feedback score, but if you stick to low-value coins you won't be losing out on much potential money either.

Buyers are not required to leave feedback after a sale, and don't always leave it—sending the buyer a friendly email with a request for feedback may help you get feedback. Make sure not to chase them too much.

Before trying to sell more valuable coins, I would recommend hitting a feedback score of at least 10 (this is the bare minimum) but the higher you can get it, the better.

Photography

Once you've got your feedback score in a good place, the next step is to create a high-quality listing. One of the most important things to sell successfully on E-bay are your photos.

Ideally, you have a DSLR or a digital camera, but at the bare minimum, you'll want something (even a smartphone) with a macro zoom function. The macro function will allow you to zoom in close to the coin while keeping it in focus.

I highly recommend buying a copy stand like the one below to hold your camera. Serviceable copy stands can be found on Amazon or eBay for $50 or less, though nicer ones will cost a couple hundred. You need a copy stand to hold your camera steady so that you can take a photo without flash while still keeping the coin in focus. A tripod can also work, though it isn't quite as versatile as a copy stand.

You'll want to take the picture on a neutral background, either black or white (I prefer white), so that the coin stands out. I recommend putting the coin on something like a marker cap or a cork so that it's elevated and separated from the background—otherwise, the camera may partially focus on the background rather than focusing entirely on the coin.

Lighting is also very important. You want consistent lighting—I prefer using two to three lamps with compact fluorescent (CFL) bulbs in a natural daylight hue, setting the lamps at the 10:00, 12:00, and 2:00 positions around the coin. LED bulbs are also great.

A normal halogen/incandescent lightbulb will impact the white balance of your picture (skewing it orange/red), so make sure you have your camera set to the correct white balance setting. (Using a natural daylight hue CFL bulb as I do means that you won't have to worry about setting the white balance, and the bulb also won't get nearly as hot as a typical halogen).

If you don't want to geek out about coin photography as much as I have and would prefer a simpler method, a single desk lamp at the 12:00 position is fine. It's better if you have something where you can point the bulb down towards the coin (like a gooseneck lamp), as an upright bulb with a lamp shade makes for more imprecise lighting.

Set the coin so that it's centered within the photo view, then set the timer delay function on your camera. This will ensure that you don't bump the camera slightly and hurt the focus when taking the picture.

Once all is set, take the picture. Try adjusting the lighting and take several pictures to figure out the optimal settings for your particular setup.

If you're using an iPhone or a phone camera, much of the above won't apply. Just try to hold your hands as steady as possible while taking the shot, and don't use the flash. Flash will result in a poorly lit photo that looks way different than the coin's actual appearance.

To illustrate the benefits of these photo tips, below are a few photos I've snapped myself.

Title

Once you've got the photos, you'll want to design the listing itself. First off, be as descriptive as possible in the title. The more relevant keywords you have in the title, the more traffic you'll get from buyers searching and finding your coin.

At the bare minimum, you should include the following:

- Date and mintmark
- Nation (i.e., U.S., France)

- Series (i.e., Walking Liberty, Morgan)
- Denomination (i.e., Nickel, Dollar)
- Condition (i.e., Mint State, Fine)
- Grade (whether the coin was professionally graded by a company like NGC or PCGS)

I also like to include the composition of the metal (if silver or gold), any descriptors specific to the coin (toned, proof-like, etc.), and any other keywords I think a buyer might use to find my coin.

Here are a few examples of well-optimized titles:

1926-S U.S. Walking Liberty Silver Half Dollar, Mint State Uncirculated Condition

1913-P U.S. Buffalo Nickel, NGC F-12 Condition

1881-S U.S. Morgan Silver Dollar, PCGS MS-63 Condition, Rainbow Toning

Product Description

The other part of the listing is the product description. Here you should give a brief description of the coin, highlighting its strong points and calling out any problem areas. Personally, I like to describe the level of wear on the coin, and describe the patina or toning. If it's an uncirculated coin, I'll also describe the strength of the luster.

Basically, what you're trying to do is give the buyer as much information as if they were able to look at the coin in hand, helping to remove the uncertainty that comes with online coin buying. You want to make the buyer confident that the coin they receive won't surprise them—that's why it's especially important to call out any problem areas such as rim dings or scratches, just in case the buyer didn't notice them in the photos.

When listing a certain coin, you may also find it helpful to search through sold listings. Look at the listings of similar coins that sold for the highest prices—how did those sellers title their coins, and what did they write in their product descriptions? You can so much lot by checking the listings of coin sellers who do this for a living.

Pricing

Starting auction price is another consideration, though less important than you might think. As long as the starting price is well below the market value of the coin, you can expect at least a decent level of bidding activity. Most coin sellers set their starting price at $0.99, which gives ample room for buyers to bid before the coin hits its market value.

Ideally, you want multiple buyers to get into a bidding war and become fixated on winning the coin, driving the price up. Bidding wars are easier to drive when you set a low starting price.

eBay also allows sellers to set a "Reserve Price" on their auctions, a price that must be reached for the coin to sell. If bidders don't bid the coin up to that price, the listing will end and the seller will keep the coin with no sale.

This may seem like an appealing option to sellers who want a bit more security with their auction listings, but I highly recommend against it. The listing will be labelled as a Reserve Price auction on the webpage, and eBay buyers generally stay away from auctions with reserves. It's unlikely that you'll get enough bidding activity to hit the Reserve Price, even if it's set very low.

CHAPTER 7

YOU ARE NOT ALONE!

Do you remember when at the beginning of this book I asked you why do you want to start coin collecting? I hope that reading this book made you think about how and why you want to start collecting coins. To help you in your journey, I prepared a few pages that described the three most common types of coin collectors that I personally met in my life. I invite you to read the next pages thinking about your goals with coin collecting and if you are taking this hobby seriously and you are committed to become "the most serious coin collector in the field" or if you just enjoy being the "common coin collector". Don't feel any pressure when going through the categories because despite the group you aspire to be part of, you will find a golden rule at the end of this small chapter!

Let's quickly look at them:

Common Coin Collector

The most common collectors or those who collect on a whim

You'll recognize yourself as a member of this group if:

- Regardless of your age, you had coins in your collection.
- You gathered at random, with no real plan.
- You don't spend too much money on coin care or purchases.
- You may find obsolete coins, coins with errors, and coins that are no longer in circulation.

A Second-Level or Curious Collector

If any of the following bullet points apply to you, you may fall into this category:

- You collect coins because you enjoy the hobby rather than because someone gave you a coin collection kit as a gift.
- You do spend money on adding to your coin collection by purchasing new coins.
- You frequently go to car dealerships to see what new commons they have to offer.
- You do spend some time searching the internet for coins on sites like eBay.
- You don't have a clear goal in mind for your collection.
- You want to always learn about coin collecting and are considering doing so on the go, such as with a note or a level.

The Most Serious Collector in the Field

If any of the following things apply to you, you can put yourself in this category:

- You devote a lot of time and energy to this regal pastime
- You're the type of collector who wants variety, and you're always on the lookout for new places to get coins from. At the very least, you want to finish a series.
- You'd rather finish one, as these have a number of unfinished series
- If you don't have enough resources, you choose what you have and finish that series.

Given that you are just starting out, it is likely that you will fall under the first or the second category at first. However, as you become more experienced, you might want to "upgrade" to the third category, depending on your budget and your specific goals as a collector.

You don't need to have an answer now, but you will need to have one if you decide to follow the golden rule of coin collecting, which is very simple and it consists of joining a coin club. Yes, the best coin collectors are all active members of clubs because it does not only help you to contact other people that share this passion but because being a member of a coin club has so many advantages and you can't exclude yourself from success and fun!

Joining a Coin Club

Individuals take part in social exercises for some reasons; most basic is partaking in a similar intrigue and enthusiasm as others. It is in places like these that data on a specific subject is shared and new thoughts and patterns are uncovered that stay up with the latest recent developments that occur in that club.

A currency assortment club is an equivalent. Since the quantity of individuals who have been doing currency gathering has expanded throughout the years, the huge system includes various clubs in a few states. In these clubs' novices and experts can share, exchange and offer new things to add to their current assortments.

There will never be an off-base chance to join a club. The difficult part is searching for one. You can begin by approaching the nearby coin vendor for help.

Some coin clubs can even be discovered on the web and will require a participation fee to be paid. Coin clubs regularly can likewise be found in the paper particularly when occasions are publicized that welcome general society to come and visit the display.

On the off chance that an individual is as yet making some hard memories finding a coin club at that point ask at the neighborhood library or the Office of Business as they might be capable of assistance giving data.

One advantage of being a part is that it is simpler to discover somebody who will purchase coins at a decent cost. Or on the other hand, maybe different individuals might need to leave behind a portion of their coins in return (called bargaining) for different coins. Most nearby coin stores just have a restricted choice that is accessible for exchanging.

Another advantage of turning into a part is to get articles that include a specific currency assortment or find better methods of thinking about an assortment. The club likewise educates its individuals about forthcoming occasions so the individual can prepare to have the option to go to the occasions.

Coin clubs are framed with the goal that each and every individual who cherishes coins can have a fabulous time. This implies it isn't just for the individuals who have an assortment at home; it is available to tenderfoots, experienced gatherers who have done it for a considerable length of time, just as currency specialists fabricate a system that empowers authorities to help others. To turn into an individual from a club simply locate an appropriate one and join the good times!

CHAPTER 8

FAKE COINS AND SCAMS

When I chose to write this book I decided to include a chapter on fake coins and scams because in the last years they have been growing significantly and even the most experienced coin collectors sometimes fall into the trap of scammers. The most and foremost important weapon you can use against scams is experience. Indeed, by acquiring experience and becoming more knowledgeable it will be more difficult to be scammed. However, sometimes this is not enough and I think you should start to understand now how to spot fake coins.

The overall process of making fake coins is quite easy to understand. A special device does the coin stamping to make them real. Individuals who counterfeit coins are well trained and have the capability to manipulate those uncommon coins, which have high worth amongst collectors. The most typical process in counterfeiting is putting fluid metal into molds, which are going to leave die marks with breaking on the fake coin.

Those who are professionals in identifying fake coins have actually observed that the modifications seen in the coins have actually added, eliminated, and even changed the coin's date markings. If an individual believes that he remains in the ownership of a fake collectible coin, he can attempt to get his other collections that are supposed to be authentic and have identical worth. He could then contrast the two coins to see whether there are any markings on the fake one.

If the coin's worth is more than 5 cents, search for corrugations in the external coin edges. These are really thin railings on the edges of the coin. They additionally call this "reeding." Authentic coins have extremely thin edges, and they are uniformly distinct if one is really watchful. Those coins which are fake could be differentiated if the edges are not sufficiently thin.

Should there be circumstances in which an individual has actually received a fake coin, he must not return the fake coin to the individual that sent it to him. He needs to attempt to delay the individual in any circumstance. If the individual runs, he needs to attempt to keep him in sight. He ought to remember the individual's clothing and physical look and attempt to remember if the individual has any buddies throughout the exchange. If they have a vehicle, get the vehicle's plate number and call the nearby authorities for assistance right away.

How to Recognize Fake Coins?

There are numerous things that could be taken into consideration when recognizing whether the coin is fake or not:

1. A coin restrike could be used to recognize verified coins. These coins are really dated earlier than those initially released by the nation that launched them with identical or specific features such as those coins, which are original.
2. Coins of a particular nation in ancient times are, in some cases, copied by another nation. An individual might believe that it is a forgery; however, it is not due to the fact that they would have been lawfully authorized in the nation where they came from.
3. Forgery could be related to a profit. It may be the primary goal of the counterfeiting syndicate. The federal government often utilizes forgery for certain political propaganda, such as in the Second World War. The Germans created countless British and American banknotes with the intent of making money from them and destabilizing the opponent's financial circumstances.

4. Another recognized kind of fake coins are the replica coins. Replica merely suggests that the initial coins are copied with identical functions and markings. Nevertheless, the typical fake coins have their distinctions that can be found by professionals. Some deliberately place the word "copy" on the sides of the coins. The majority of these replicas are utilized for academic functions and museum displays.

5. The Lebanese connection is stated to have a big creation of fake coins. These coins were discovered to be utilized to trick lots of museums, business leaders, collectors and other nations which are looking for their ancient lost coins.

6. The circulated intended forgery and the collector intended forgery are kinds of forgeries where the coin worth is token intended, and the face values are accepted, despite their illegality and intrusive, unimportant values.

If you want to be really sure if a coin is fake or not you should consider seeing a professional. An experienced individual with years of experience in this sector could quickly find the incorrect metal utilized for counterfeiting. If the individual is a collector of such products, he ought to be more familiar with these coins. A collector has to be more worried about the uncommon collectible coins due to the fact that this is where counterfeiters gain. They go for the really valuable market where they could make money.

Tips on How to Stay Away From Scams

Lots of people delight in shopping on the web, where there are fantastic coins, which could be discovered. An individual might do his shopping while he is at house due to the fact that it is so hassle-free and time-saving instead of heading out searching for shops, which offer collectible coins and other keepsakes.

An individual can distinguish a live auction from those on the Web since live auctions entertain bidders, who call for the greatest price when the time comes. Lots of people which are bidding on the web make their experience so enjoyable, and they are familiar with the techniques on how they would win a web auction.

There are online websites where an individual could purchase any product that might catch his/her interest. This is where many coin collectors buy their preferred coins. By browsing and discovering the product that they desire, they could, in fact, negotiate and make the payments via the Web.

Even though it could be too risky to rely on a seller who is unidentified to the purchaser, many individuals are still making deals and payments via this sort of online auction.

Fraud is usually frequent nowadays, though numerous internet sites that do business online claim that the danger of fraud is not a thing to stress over. They state that just 0.0025 percent of real instances of fraud occur online. That implies only that one out of 40,000 noted web deals might be a fraud. On the other hand, the FBI has its own investigations, which show that the figures are not correct. They claim that the danger of fraud is a lot greater according to their stats.

An individual ought to trust the FBI for this protection. Even though one can state that most online coin selling is all truthful and reliable, the procedure in which the deal is made could be most likely doubtful and unpredictable. There are business deals, which are directly carrying out fraud. Aside from flea market dealers, in-person auctions, mail-order sellers and some coin shops, the Web has the best odds of pulling off a fraud.

One protection that a coin purchaser ought to be aware of is how to make "feedback." By doing this, an individual could see the scores of other bidders, and he might compare his deal with the deals of the others. In case there is a great likelihood of fraud with negative feedback, the individual might withdraw his involvement in the auction.

An individual might additionally get ideas by trying to find those members who have actually left "positive feedback" and compare it to the seller's response. An individual can make an evaluation of what may be feasible helpful information from those responses. An individual should be cautious when it comes to any deal which is offered.

There are circumstances in which an individual is tricked into buying the product. The picture on the Internet showed the coin that individual wishes to have; however, they delivered something else entirely. These cases resemble fraud. An individual needs to ensure that the product he saw in the picture is the same product that is going to be shipped to him. Here are some suggestions that are going to assist an individual in preventing fraud throughout a coin search on the web.

- An individual ought to save the online image of the coin he wishes to buy. There are sellers who get rid of the title and the image of the product when a purchase has actually been made.
- An individual ought to get the auction information and the description. It could either be e-mailed to the individual or sent out by means of postal mail.
- If there are doubts concerning the auction, an individual ought to request an explanatory note. This is going to prevent misunderstanding and confusion on the part of the purchaser.
- An individual can decline any deal where he believes the price offered on the coin is too much. One ought to know the market price of the particular coin and contrast it to the price which was offered throughout the online transaction.

These are just a few pointers that are going to guarantee an individual his safety when making any deals online. Fraud could occur to anybody, specifically those who have an interest in buying collectible coins online. It is essential to be informed and updated on the possibilities of coming across a fraud.

COIN COLLECTING FOR BEGINNERS

CHAPTER 9

SHOWING YOUR COIN COLLECTION

Coin Shows

Coin shows open a lot of opportunities for all those involved in numismatics. They draw a lot of interest from buyers, sellers, and dealers who all join hands to come up with an event where everyone concerned can learn and acquire something new. If you are attending your very first show, be warned that you could find it quite overwhelming. But give yourself a little time and you will certainly go where the rest are going.

It is in these events where coin seekers find the holy grail of coins—the long lost very rare coins that they have long wanted to possess. Buyers who are eager to finally purchase the coin that will complete their set will welcome the presence of hundreds of sellers who could provide what they want.

The sellers and dealers alike will surely welcome too, the attendance of thousands of buyers who are ready to part with their money and write checks to purchase their coins. But coin shows are not merely venues where you can see valuable rare coins, both ancient and modern displayed in showcases and are for sale. It is also the place where you can learn a lot about this hobby of kings that started hundreds of years ago through exhibits, seminars and talks presented by numismatic experts.

As a novice coin collector, you might not know what to do or how to deal with sellers and dealers if you are going to buy coins, whether as an investment or to add to your growing collection.

Dealers who attend coin shows are kept current on numismatic events and thus are expected to give better service to their clients. They also have a network consisting of other dealers who are equally updated. This translates to a better relationship with you as a client because you may someday want to buy a particular coin, and the dealer might know just which dealer to contact.

Pointers on How to Attend Coin Shows

Attending coin shows is beneficial to both collectors and dealers. So, if you are intent on growing and learning more, it is imperative that you attend one. If you have just started in this great hobby, you still might not know when and where coin shows are held.

One way to solve this predicament is to become a member of coin clubs where you can get such information. Coin clubs offer opportunities to meet other collectors like you who will be willing to show you the ropes and perhaps become your mentor. You can also find where and when coins show will be held in your local newspapers. If you don't have problems with the Internet, you can also go to websites that offer this kind of information.

- Before going to a coin show, make sure that you have already decided what you want to sell or buy. It will help focus your energies and let you avoid impulse buying or selling coins you never wanted to sell at all. You have to determine how much you are willing to spend on each coin.
- Searching for coins you want takes hours so you have to give yourself time for this purpose. There are plenty of dealers' tables that are waiting for you to browse and pick on the merchandise. You might want to find out more about the coin from the seller and take your time mulling over the planned purchase. They would only be too glad to assist you in making

the final decision to buy. And if the dealer seems upset by your queries, simply walk away and go to the next dealer.

- If you are after a particular coin, it will help if you already have some knowledge about that coin beforehand. With a small preparation before the show, you can save a lot of frustration and money as well. You need to know, for example, what is considered a reasonable price for the coins. Knowing the correct name and description of the coins you want won't hurt either. You can read references, catalogs, and price lists for this information. Some of these are available online too. This will expedite the transaction as the dealer will only have to confirm what you already know about the coin. It may happen that the coin you wanted is not even on display at any of the dealers' tables. You may ask the dealers and usually, they can direct you to somebody else who would probably know where you can find it.

- If you are selling you will also need time to talk with other dealers and show them what you have. Start with a high price but be prepared to negotiate. Be realistic however as seldom will you get the full published price. When a dealer happens to like what you are selling and makes an offer, be sure you can decide immediately. The dealer will not trust you to come back later because a dishonest seller could substitute fewer valuable items than the one shown earlier.

- Cash is the most common way of payment for your purchases. Many dealers will not accept personal checks. They won't accept credit cards simply because they are not set up for such transactions. Usually, there are ATMs in the venue but bear in mind that they may run out of cash or charge high fees.

- Haven't you noticed that coin shows are fun! The fun part comes from learning new things as you look around at the collectors' exhibits and attend seminars or educational programs that are presented, with participation from coin lovers all over.

- Remember you are attending a show where the bourse floor is located in a huge venue where you will have to do a lot of walking. So put on a comfortable pair of shoes and equally comfortable clothing so you can fully enjoy the experience.

- Be considerate and please don't bring a spouse, a child or a friend who is not interested, although you can always try to convert them to being a coin collector like you! I tried but only a few times actually work)

- Always ask for permission from the dealer before handling their coins, (always by the edges) especially if they are not in a protective holder or if they are in a display case.

- Dealers' tables can become overcrowded, whether in a major show or a local one. If you're just browsing and undecided whether to buy or not, be sure to give way to those who are buying. Make sure that you are not holding on to any coin when you move.

- You might not have even bought a coin you have been looking for to complete a set in your collection but it doesn't mean that it was all for nothing and that you were unsuccessful. You are not even obligated to buy anything at all. Remember, coins shows are meant to be enjoyed, especially in the company of like-minded people.

Coin Show Etiquette

People tend to overreact when they are overwhelmed. You have been warned that attending your first coin show can overwhelm you. So, you would do good to start learning how you have to behave in a coin show. Nothing here is hard to do, but it takes a lot of common sense to make it work and let you survive your first ever coin show.

Coin shows can also be intimidating for the first-time attendee. It is not unknown however for regular coin show attendees frequently lose their bearing and break some coin show etiquette. They do things that may be considered as "unbecoming a numismatist".

Proper Perspective: The Coin Dealers' Point of View

You are a coin collector out to get your very first coin. You are very eager to look at and handle every coin you fancy as the one you want and then you realize that it is not. So, you pick up another, and then another. You may not notice it at this point but for sure, the dealer is looking at you, very nervously, trying to catch your every move.

The reason? It is because the dealer is apprehensive about potential losses since the coins in front of you are presumably the dealer's best and thus, the most expensive in his collection. Therefore, the first thing you have to keep in mind is to put the dealer's fears aside: that you are not there to make off with his valuable coins. Put him at ease by not making any move that the dealer can interpret as stealing.

Put Those Bags and Purses Away

You wouldn't want the dealer to think that you are squirreling his coins into your purse. Keep your hands free and open to view. This way, the dealer will not think you are doing something you shouldn't be doing. When you need to sit down, put your bag or purse on the back of your chair, on the floor or under the chair, but never on your lap or in front of you. Again, the point here is to look at things from the dealer's point of view: You wouldn't want your customers dropping your coins onto their bags or purses, which is what the dealer will think if you put your bag in your lap or in front of you where you can simply drop a coin at the right time.

Pick the Best but Be Sure You Know Where You Picked It

There is a term in the numismatic hobby that best describes how a collector finds a coin: cherry-picking. The term is based on the process of harvesting cherries where the picker is expected to select only the ripest and healthiest fruit. Applied to coin collecting, it is the art of buying the best possible coin at the lowest price. This means going through a bunch of coins in the box and trying to find the valuable one among the worthless ones. But it often happens that someone would forget where they picked up the coin and just put it back wherever they could. This leads to confusion and embarrassment if the coin is not returned to its original container, especially if the price of the coin is different, either higher or lower, than the one it originally came from.

Beware: Bury Those Books and Checklists

It is an acceptable practice to bring reference books like "the Red Book", so you could consult their pages and be properly informed about the prices. However, you should not bring them out when you are actually looking and handling the coins. Remember to consider this scene from the dealer's point of view again: you could easily slip coins between pages or slips of paper. You are not going to do that of course, but the dealer might think you will. So don't let any coins near your books and papers.

Show Me Your Hands!

Don't blame the dealer for thinking that you are out to get his coins! For sure, the dealer would have had past experiences along this line. You know it is very easy to palm coins and drop them into your purse, bag or pockets and not get noticed at all. So, stop giving the dealer a reason to suspect that you are out to pocket his coins. Always show your hands palms up and if you have to take out something from your purse or pocket, tell the dealer what you are about to do. If you have been picking up coins (remember to hold them by the edge) you want to buy, and have to move to give way to other customers, let the dealer hold the coins for you. Never for a moment, (this is essential for your survival in your first coin show or any subsequent show for that matter) step away from the dealer's table with coins you haven't paid yet. You do not want the dealer to think that you are stealing his coins. People have been thrown out of coin shows this way.

Displaying Your Coin Collection

You certainly are proud of your collection. It may not be large at this point but you are making progress and you want to show it off. You can use display cases, boxes, even picture frames, folders and presentation binders. At home, you can use a bookcase or cabinet to display your coins. You may set up either a permanent display or only for special occasions. The thing to bear in mind is to make it as attractive as possible. You can also use the same setup if in the future, you want to sell your collection.

Use attractive leather or vinyl coin albums or sleeves to display your American coins. Look at online stores for custom albums to display American dimes, pennies, and nickels. For your special favorite coins, your best bet is to display them in a wooden cabinet with trays, preferably with velvet linings.

If you are preparing your coins to be displayed in a coin show, whether as exhibit pieces or for sale, you can follow what many collectors do with their prized possessions. They place their coins inside a coin collecting album which displays the coins in all their splendid state. This type of album is not made to be coin holders and then hidden in an obscure drawer somewhere in the house. Rather it is meant to be displayed and seen. Coins in a collecting album attract attention as it shows the beauty and details of the coins for everyone to see.

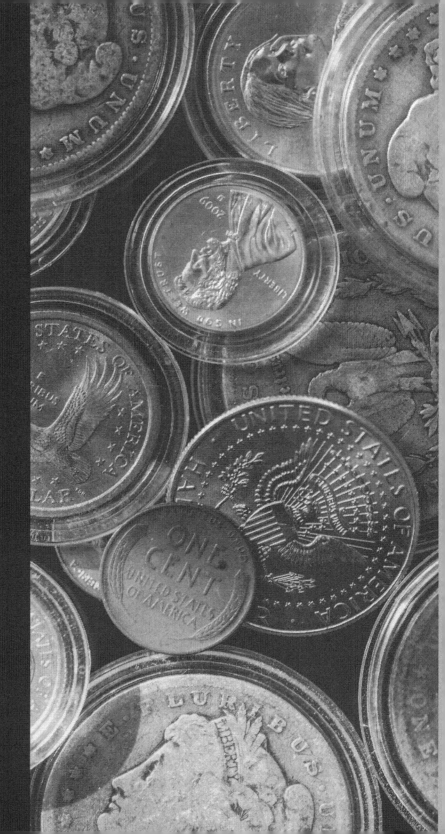

COIN COLLECTING FOR BEGINNERS

CONCLUSION

People approach coin collecting for numerous reasons. Some collect due to the fact that they find the historic nature of the pastime really intriguing. Don't forget that every coin is a real piece of the daily life of individuals who lived decades, even centuries back. These coins were used by the hands of countless individuals, a few of whom might even be individuals you had heard of.

Coin Collecting is also an investment. Investing in coins is a very simple approach to diversify an individual's financial portfolio. It is a simple approach to hedge against inflation as well as economic uncertainty. It should be noted that the greatest risk with investing in coins is the market for rare collectibles can be extremely volatile. Some people collect because they wish to pass along their legacy, and finding the best coin collection book or CD in order to do so is not really difficult.

There are numerous resources intended for collectors of all skill levels such as magazines and online resources. Coin collecting books are extremely popular among enthusiasts and collectors. A lot of people who collect coins have no formal education in it whatsoever. There are also coin clubs, which can play an important role in helping you expand your knowledge base, while also providing you with the latest information on collectible coins. Don't forget that equipment and other coin collectors are your best asset.

A huge aspect of ending up being an effective coin collector is to learn about it and constantly discover brand-new information as it appears. Sign up with a local coin club in case there is one in your area. Try to find coin collecting groups online. This could be a significant networking chance for you and the opportunity to discover somebody who has a coin you desire. The more individuals you know who enjoy coin collecting, the more chances you are going to have to contribute to your collection and maybe make a bit of cash too. Remember that knowledge and experience are essential to be successful in coin collecting.

Additionally, a lot of people collect pieces they feel have particular value or significance to them. These are generally referred to as "investment coins" and may be worth more than face value. Collecting investment coins is a legitimate area to earn money in the coin market also.

Coin collecting has been a fun and rewarding pastime for ages. It only takes a little research and knowledge to end up being an experienced collector who can find the best deals for coins and rare collectibles.

Coin Collecting is not simply about accumulating coins, it is about discovering and learning about history through coins, as well as other collectibles, without even stepping foot outside your home.

I hope that you enjoyed reading through this book and that you now feel a little bit more ready to start your journey into coin collecting.